Be A
Great Thinker

Socrates: **Man, Myth, Teacher**

A Young Adult's Introduction

Book 2

Adrienne Roth & Matthew Roth

Wolf Lake Press

ISBN: 979-8-9861552-0-3

Contents

ACKNOWLEDGMENTS

Book Cover Created by Mahabuba Akter

Book Layout Designed by Olivia Stone

1

SO, WHO WAS The Great Thinker Socrates?

"We can easily forgive a child who is afraid of the dark; the real tragedy of life is when men are afraid of the light."

-Socrates

So, who was Socrates, and why does he still matter?

As the quote above reflects, he was a man who believed that we, as humans, must become enlightened and must learn all we can learn about the world. You may have heard his name at school, in books, on television, or the internet. Socrates (pronounced Sock-rat-EEZ) is one in a group of famous Greek philosophers, and of those philosophers, he is among three mentioned frequently

Socrates, Plato, and Aristotle of those three, Socrates came first.

What makes him so important, and why should we care about him today?

Good questions that deserve good answers.

Socrates was a bit of a rabble-rouser. He caused a copious amount of trouble, so much so that he was eventually tried, found guilty, and sentenced to death for his views. The man took risks in a society that did not appreciate those risks. He was a man ahead of his time in a backward world. When you are that kind of person, your words and actions can make a difference. His words certainly did. However, he paid the ultimate price for it.

What makes him so important? He is considered the first philosopher to introduce critical thinking methods. We still follow many of the techniques he introduced in his life and teachings a few thousand years ago. And why should we care today what he taught so many years ago? Knowing Socrates, his point of view, and his philosophies give you an excellent base to understand critical thinking. He established the way we should conduct critical thinking; you might even have heard of it in passing – the Socratic Method. We will delve further into the Socratic Method later in this book.

Socrates was a teacher of his philosophies; however, he never documented any of his teachings; instead, his teachings were reflected by his students like Plato. Still, his teachings resonate today.

Come with us to discover who Socrates was, what he taught, and what he said, and immerse yourself in a few critical thinking exercises that reflect how you perceive the world. But first, let us read more about the life and views of the great thinker Socrates.

2

—⌖—

A Very Brief Biography of Socrates

—⌖—

Socrates was born in Athens, Greece, in 469 BC. His father was a stonemason. His mother was a midwife. His family was not poor, but they were also not wealthy. Unlike his friends and compatriots, Socrates did not come from the nobility. His father had enough wealth to get Socrates a good education. And a good education was essential to being part of Athenian society.

He studied essential Athenian topics in school, like reading, writing, poetry, and music. He was very active in a variety of sports while at school. It is unknown how good a student he was, but there is no doubt he probably challenged his teachers often.

After he left school, Socrates served in the military. He did well in the military as a soldier.

Socrates fought in the First Peloponnesian War that started in 460 BC. He fought against Sparta in this war.

Sparta and Athens were the largest cities in ancient Greece at the time, and this war shifted the power of Athens to Sparta. The war weakened Greece for a long time, and Athens lost its dominance in the region. The shift in power in Greece eventually led to the rise of Alexander the Great, although his rise would come several decades later.

Socrates appreciated beautiful people, especially since he wasn't considered handsome. He was often made fun of because of his looks. They said he had a flat, turned-up nose, bulging eyes, a big belly, and he wore a ragged coat that he rarely washed. He never took a bath and liked walking the streets of Athens barefooted.

He was not concerned about this, and it didn't hinder his personal life. He was married twice, and he had three sons.

From his earliest days, Socrates loved learning. He was brilliant, and he questioned everything and everyone, which often got him into trouble, especially when he questioned his superiors at school or in the military. Those in his society did not appreciate his questioning ways.

But he used this kind of persistent questioning to teach the very bright youth of Athens. He strove to have them do the same type of questioning when trying to comprehend the world. He would never give answers to their questions. Instead, he expected his students to come up with their own conclusions.

Socrates never wrote down any of his ideas. It never occurred to him to do so. But he affected the thinking of two of his students so much that they wrote down Socrates' philosophies in their own words. These two philosophers were Plato and Xenophon.

In Socrates' time, Athens had two political factions: The Democrats and the Oligarchs.

Democrat   **Oligarch**

In ancient Greek society, Democrats believed in a government ruled by the people, where the citizens could create and vote on laws. Not everyone at that time thought democracy was a good idea. They felt that people could be corrupted into creating bad laws that would have the possibility of benefiting a privileged few. An Oligarchy was a city-state ruled by a handful of men who claimed power for themselves and ruled like kings. Oligarchs made laws that benefited the wealthy and hurt the poor. They also used the military to enforce their laws. Both sides had their supporters and their detractors.

Socrates did not like either group. He disliked politics altogether. Much like factions throughout the world today, the two parties in Greece were at odds. There was a great deal of division, and both sides fought constantly. Socrates chose to stay away from this conflict, not wanting any part of it. Yet, Socrates was very respectful of Athenian laws, which the Democrats primarily created. However, he sympathized with the Oligarchs, as most of his friends were Oligarchs. Still, he argued about the ideals of democracy and what it meant to be in a democratic society.

There were two frames of thought as to who Socrates was aligned. We don't know which is accurate. Some say that he aligned with the elitist Oligarchs, while others argued that he sided with the more high-minded Democrats. He believed that a person should be free to come and go as they please, but they also must accept the city's laws, as this was the best way to live in a society. It was a high-minded idea for his time.

Socrates was possibly the first person to use civil disobedience in society. Though he felt citizens should follow the laws of their state, if, after some reflection on those laws, they found them to be unjust, then it was their duty as a citizen to fight against those unjust laws.

Part of Socrates's civil disobedience came in his persistence to remain teaching his students despite being ordered to stop by the authorities. Socrates believed he was a man of high principles. Thus, he broke what he felt was an unjust law, as he thought what he taught his students was significant.

In 399 BC, after years of teaching his philosophies to the bright youth of Athens, Socrates was put on trial for corrupting the minds of these youth with what was considered "deviant thinking." Though he did try to defend himself, he was found guilty of corrupting the youth and not practicing the state religion, which alone was considered a terrible crime. In Athens, there was no tolerance for anyone who went against the norms of Greek society.

Socrates had the opportunity to flee from his prison to safety. His friends pleaded with him to take that chance. They tried to get him to bribe the prison guards and escape to the city of Thessaly, where he could live out the remainder of his life in peace. But Socrates refused

"Death of Socrates"

to do this. Instead, he spent the rest of his days visited by friends, awaiting his punishment.

Socrates chose to follow the laws and not do the easy thing by escaping. He instead took his punishment bravely, drinking the poison hemlock, which was what took his life.

His words, thoughts, and philosophies touched the world only after his death. But because of his effect on his students, they let the rest of the world know who Socrates was. Millennia later, he is still teaching all of us. He is forever considered one of the most outstanding teachers of all time.

What do you think of Socrates' behavior throughout his life?

Do you think being an outsider in Greek society was essential to Socrates becoming a great thinker?

Can you relate to Socrates? Do you always follow the norms, or do you try to think outside the box and find the answers for yourself?

—❦—

Socrates, the Myth, The Mystery and the Teacher

—❦—

As Socrates never wrote anything down, what we know about him comes from second-hand knowledge. The brunt of his life, work, and ideas came from dialogs written by his student, Plato, or reflected on by other philosophers. Plato was considered the Father of Western Philosophy, and he was deeply influenced by his teacher, Socrates.

Socrates was the philosopher that believed that we must question everything. We should not take anything at face value and must separate fact from fiction or opinion.

This concept of questioning everything was essential to how Socrates approached society and was integral to what he taught his impressionable students, like Plato.

Socrates was a mystery, even to some degree a myth, created by others who felt compelled to tell his life story and reveal what they thought was his most important ideas and concepts. The reflections of his students have elevated Socrates, and to this day, he is considered one of the most outstanding teachers ever to exist. His students were compelled to introduce the world to his concepts, which caught fire. Some thought his ideas needed to be seriously contemplated, and his ideas would ultimately become part of the mainstream, especially regarding philosophy and critical thinking.

But what we don't quite know is if Socrates would have appreciated having his ideas imparted to the world. Had he wanted this, he would have likely written them down. He was a modest man and lived a simple life, so fame was not necessarily something he sought or accepted. Again, even this is just speculation. Truthfully, all we can impart about Socrates is speculation, as he never gave his perspective and point of view in his own words. But the legacy that Socrates left is said to be profound. Many people view Socrates as a saint, a great man who lived far above mere mortals.

Yet how others have seen him throughout the centuries only adds to the factor of how mysterious Socrates was. Some people have considered him equal to a religious figure, expressing views similar to a deity. This likely would have thrown Socrates for a loop, as part of the reason for his guilty verdict and death sentence was due partially to him not following the state-sanctioned religion. He was humble and likely would not have appreciated being considered God-like.

Many of Socrates' ideas caused conflict among various philosophers, as many different kinds of philosophers have claimed him as one of their own. He doesn't fit into one category, and philosophers like the skeptics, the stoics, the cynics, spiritualists, and humanists all have felt that they followed his philosophies the best. They believed he spoke for them and their ideologies. They thought they were purists when it came to Socrates. His Socratic Method is used by scholars, philosophers, and scientists alike and is considered the pinnacle for breaking down an argument. His appeal ranges to many ideologies, which is why he is so popular.

What is known about Socrates was that he lived in a time of political upheaval. Yet, in the middle of this political division, Socrates took the opportunity to open the minds of his students. He did not take sides and taught his students how to view each side of the argument and not be driven by bias but by fact. That is his most incredible legacy and, to a great extent, his biggest downfall, as this was what led to his arrest, trial, and conviction.

Socrates' words and concepts had philosophers from as early as Plato and Aristotle to the philosophers of the Middle Ages, the Renaissance period, the Existentialists, and the modern-day questioning their own well-examined beliefs. They used his method to hone their arguments. Socrates continues to be a great teacher in this respect. This is where man, myth, and teacher become one.

4

—ल/ठ—

The Socratic Method, OR Questioning Everything

—ल/ठ—

"Answer all the questions. Question all the answers."
Laurie Gray

A story is told about Socrates where the Oracle of Delphi was once asked, for whom is the wisest man in all of Greece? The Oracle then replied, "Socrates is the wisest man."

All the men in the land took this statement very seriously. Even Socrates, who was skeptical, had no choice but to take this decree seriously. Still, he was surprised by the declaration. Socrates could only admit to the Oracle's proclamation by saying this, "I am the wisest man alive, for I know one thing, that I know nothing."

In Socrates' time, many men professed to be well-educated and experts at something or another. These men were considered with reverence. But few of these men could maintain their ideas against Socrates' persistent questioning. This, in turn, made Socrates quite skeptical as to the claims they made, as their arguments often could not stand up to his examinations of them. His constant questions did not make Socrates very popular among the elites of his society.

Socrates created a method of questioning an assertion or an idea, and he presented this method to his students. His desire was not to win an argument but to challenge how the statement is made and bring it down to its core.

Socrates found a way to get his students to break down the argument by asking questions, exposing any contradictions and flaws in the arguer's thought process. He wanted to guide his students to reach a solid conclusion by going through this process. It was a way to find holes in an argument or a theory and then patch them up.

Since Socrates did not believe that he knew all the answers, like some of his counterparts thought they did, he felt this gave him more freedom to question everything. He taught his students to never accept one answer as the be-all, end-all, but to be the base for the conclusion.

This method, also known as the Socratic Method, has become the basis of critical thinking and defines reason and logic in an argument.

Students, professionals, and others use the Socratic Method to get to the heart of an argument. Those in the legal and medical fields often use the Socratic Method to break down complex concepts, using shared dialog between students and professionals or by a series of rapid-fire questions that break down these arguments to their core. In its pure form, the Socratic Method can be both exciting and frustrating at the same time, mainly because it goes against the grain of our thought process and breaks down barriers to find the sense in things that sometimes don't make sense.

You may have trouble believing this, but you may have already used the Socratic Method as a child, especially when interacting with your parents or another authority figure.

When your parents told you that you had to "eat all of your vegetables," you may have questioned them as to why you had to do so?

"Because vegetables are good for you."

"Why are vegetables good for me?"

"Because they have all the good nutrients you need for your growing body."

"Why do I need those nutrients?"

"So, they can help you grow up strong."

"Why do I need to grow up strong?"

And the endless questions go on and on.

You would wear your parents down with rapid-fire questions until, finally, they would snap and say, "You have to eat your vegetables because I say so. Now stop asking so many questions!" And the argument would thus end, with no natural, satisfying conclusion, except that you have frustrated your parents, and you still must eat the less than delightful broccoli on your plate. Still, you learned an essential process of questioning and this early lesson has you unknowingly tapped into the Socratic Method.

The Socratic Method is a bit more disciplined in its approach than what you might have experienced as a child. It is broken down into six steps.

Here Are the Six Steps of the Socratic Method

The first step is to hear what the other person is saying and their premise. The crucial part of this step is to listen to the other person's argument. After you hear the premise, it would be best to ask a question to figure out why they are thinking this way or why they have said this.

If someone were to come to you with a baseless argument, you might think, "What are they talking about?" This step encourages you to ask them to clarify their statement.

The second step is to probe further into their assumptions. A little more listening comes in handy, as you will start to hear the flaws in their argument, and you can respond accordingly with the appropriate questions to counter this argument.

Someone might tell you about their illogical argument, and you shake your head, stunned by what they are saying. While listening closely to their flawed premise and point of view, you pose relevant questions to challenge their theory.

The third step is to reflect on the other person's argument. You want to have them clarify their argument and then say it back to them, paraphrasing the idea. You don't need to be exact, but state what you think you heard. They also need to hear it back in your words.

This is the part where you say, "Okay, so let me get this straight...."

The fourth step is to make them provide evidence about their argument. It would help if you saw what brought them to this conclusion and why they hold this flawed understanding or idea at this point of the method. This step will bring out the assumptions of their argument rather than the facts. Here is where you start to challenge those assumptions with your questions. It would be best to break them down, and they need to withstand the questioning.

This is where you ask them, "Where did you get this idea from?"

The fifth step is to take a step back. Here you want them to either re-word their argument or adapt it to facts rather than assumptions. If it looks as though they have started to refine their thinking, then you want to re-state their new position. Has this position improved by any method, or are there still flaws to be questioned and explored?

After you have peppered them with questions and they get annoyed with you, let the other person improve and then restate their argument.

The sixth and final step is to repeat the method, as it appears they now may have a new viewpoint. You can go back to the start of the process. You can assess the unique premise and point out similar or incorrect assumptions. The idea is to rule out all the flaws in their argument entirely. Their concept may still lack substance if it cannot stand up to the questions and cannot be debunked. If there is any weakness in the argument, those weaknesses must continue to be exposed.

At this point, have them restate their new premise and acknowledge it. But if it still sounds wrong, keep asking them questions, keep debunking their belief.

The process of the Socratic Method is the way for people to step away from their built-in belief systems. It helps to view their old, flawed notions by questioning ideas that have become familiar and comfortable. It keeps a person from remaining stagnant in their thought process and opens the world to them by enabling them to see new points of view.

The Socratic Method is not the perfect way to get to an answer, and honestly, it can sometimes leave us with more questions than answers. This can leave us more confused, even frustrated by the conclusion, or lack thereof. But sometimes, with some arguments, there are no satisfying resolutions. One side does not always beat the other side. Both sides sometimes can be right in their way.

But don't let this deter you. As someone who wants to learn more about critical thinking, the answers to the most profound questions won't come quickly or may never come. You may find that something you believed in all your life and felt was the truth may be challenged by questions. If the "truth" does not remain solid, you may need to change your thinking. Also, you never want to stay with one ideology, idea, or concept.

As you grow and learn and discover more about the world, your thoughts, opinions, and beliefs should also evolve and change. You may never be one kind of person with one type of belief as you are more a part of the world.

Embrace the Socratic Method to delve deeper into a subject, an argument, or a view. Hone the skill to question flawed conclusions to better understand the world around you. It might seem complicated, but it can be satisfying when you can ask questions and keep others on their toes, showing them how to understand their arguments better.

—✧—

5

Bringing a Bit of Socrates into your life

—✧—

Socrates had many philosophies that we should all reflect on. We will review these Socratic life lessons and discover how best to implement them into your life. Each of the following quotes is attributed to Socrates.

Embracing Truth or the Socratic Paradox

"There is only one good, knowledge, and one evil, ignorance."

The quote above is an example of a Socratic Paradox. A paradox is a statement that sounds absurd or self-contradictory when heard but, when viewed closer, ends up being true in most respects.

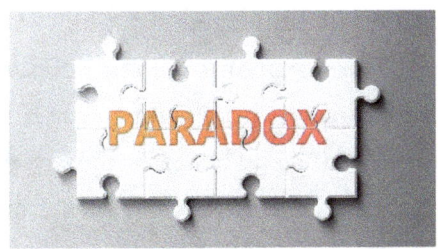

A couple of examples that Socrates and other of his followers used to explain this paradox are these:

No one wants to be evil, but sometimes they do evil things or have evil goals. This means that people do things they believe are for good but can be harmful or destructive. A perfect example of this is when books have been banned because some people feel the contents of those books are offensive to their way of thinking. Still, because they are banning those books, they, in turn, are doing a bad deed because they are silencing voices that should be heard. This kind of activity is what is called evil ignorance. They act in a manner that results in evil, though they are ignorant that their actions bring about evil. They may argue that they are correct, but we would hope they would see the error of their thinking and change their actions if presented with logic.

It is better to be the victim of an injustice than to be the one to cause the injustice. This paradox states that being a just person and doing something to fight against injustice is to be virtuous. Though, if you are the person who unconsciously pushes an injustice onto others, this means you are acting in a dishonorable manner. No one ever looks upon the bully as the hero. It is always those they bully that gain sympathy.

Both paradoxes are not simple. At any point in our lives, we can be on both sides of the argument at different times, depending on the circumstances we find ourselves in. For the most part, we will feel that we are not evil in our thinking and beliefs and that we will always stand up for the rights of others, but then we may turn around and do or say something that contradicts this. When you encounter a paradox, use your brain, and question everything. Utilize the Socratic Method to break down the argument to reveal the base of the debate. Even if it runs against your original grain of thought, try to think differently and act differently to make the situation and the world better.

The Socratic View of Having Courage in Your Life

"Be kind, for everyone you meet is fighting a hard battle."

In his time, Socrates was quite a polarizing figure. He didn't dress or act acceptably in his world. He aggravated others with his persistent and invasive questions. He was not afraid to go against the norms of Athenian beliefs and opinions.

Socrates was courageous because he knew what he felt about the world and that his actions could cause him trouble. He remained fearless to his final days because he did not relent. He stayed true to his principles, as nothing less would have sufficed in Socrates' point of view.

We learn virtuousness from Socrates' courage. He stood up for his moral principles. Do you believe you can be similarly courageous?

How do you show courage? If you aren't sure, here are a few examples:

1. Try something new, something that you might not feel comfortable doing. This could be eating something you have turned your nose up at or found unappealing. Or listen to music that you never considered listening to before.
2. Start playing a sport, even if you fail at it. Or you can try out for a role in the class play or for that solo in your music class.
3. You can stand up and make a speech on a topic that you feel passionate about, maybe just in front of friends, then in front of your class, and finally in front of the entire school.
4. Stand up and help a friend or classmate in need.
5. You can form a rally on an issue that you feel needs more attention.
6. You can stand up to the class bully.
7. You can run for your school government to help change the rules at your school.
8. You can call out someone who says or does something harmful.

You don't have to do something big to be courageous. Just being helpful or fighting against injustice is courageous. When you think of a hero, what comes to your mind? Is it a first responder jumping into action to save someone? Is it a soldier on the battlefield? Is it a freedom fighter fighting against racism and injustice? Is it a superhero like

Batman, Spiderman, or Black Panther? Or is it someone like you, taking a stand, trying to do something that can cause a positive change, or just participating in an activity you would have never thought of participating in before?

If you don't think of yourself as a hero, no one else will. But also follow the path of Socrates and lead your life by logic. Understand that you are the champion of your own story, your own life. But courage also must fall in line with responsibility and compassion for others. Try not to fall into the trap of believing you are acting on behalf of others, but in truth, working only to benefit yourself. A true champion understands all sides before acting and acts without malice.

Socrates Believed That You Should Be True to Yourself

"The greatest way to live with honor in this world is to be what we pretend to be."

Socrates was not considered a handsome man. He did not dress to impress. He lived simply, was not polished, and stayed authentic to his character throughout his life. This kind of behavior brought him both ridicule and admiration. He didn't seem interested in either opinion, as he felt that he could only be true to himself.

Being true to yourself means being authentic, not following the crowd, stopping seeking the approval of others, and not behaving in a way that is only to get likes and impress strangers that have no impact on our lives.

It can be hard to be authentic when it is more comfortable to conform to the standards of others. But it is a documented fact that trying to appear "perfect" by showing off a reality that isn't factual can bring unnecessary angst into our lives. These ideals of perfection, which we may try to achieve, compete not with an accurate picture of who we are but what we wish to be. That picture could be out of reach for most.

Instead of trying to be something you aren't, develop the person you wish to be. Don't be ruled by the judgment of others. It might seem important now to be famous or well-liked or admired, as this seems to be the way to a happier life, but if you try too hard to be something you aren't, you will never be pleased with it yourself. It truly is okay not to have the perfect figure, the perfect complexion, the best clothes, the most stuff, or the most friends. Even if you feel socially awkward around others or in group situations, this doesn't make you less. Learning to speak to people, engage them, and be comfortable with social interactions takes practice. Even those who are considered charming, and the life of the party didn't come to it naturally. They faltered a few times before they found their footing to succeed in social situations.

Suppose you struggle with your identity, sexuality, or how you fit in the world; don't worry, it's okay. You may grow up and never quite know who you are. We evolve throughout our lives.

What we feel at ten or fifteen or twenty will not be the same when we are in our thirties, forties, and beyond. We change with the times and with our experiences. You don't want to sabotage who you are in favor of others' opinions. What they believe does not matter, not really. Yes, the world does subscribe to norms, and if you fall outside those norms, others will judge you. Unfortunately, we cannot change this. What you can change is how you act or react to being judged. Do you take it personally, internalize it and then punish yourself for what others see in you, or take a deep breath and say that though it might hurt, you are not deterred, that you will not let others change who you are? You will stay authentic to yourself; not what others feel you should be.

Being truly authentic and genuine to yourself also falls under courage. It is similarly courageous to be your own person and not be ruled by what society wants or expects. Few can manage it. But work on it so that you can be one of those who can be genuinely authentic.

Be A Humble Person, Much Like Socrates

"Pride divides men; humility joins them."

Because Socrates did not care about his appearance or overthink himself, this freed him to speak with anyone willing to engage with him in conversation. He also did not discriminate against those he spoke with. Socrates found it easy to talk with men of noble standing, people of lesser circumstances, and women and enslaved people alike. It didn't matter if they were young, old, rich, or poor. He enjoyed engaging with them and hearing their opinions. Doing this made him a more well-rounded individual.

The definition of humility is a modest or low view of one's importance. It is freedom from pride or arrogance.

Being humble must be practiced. It is an under-rated virtue, not one many of us utilize. Some consider being humble an old-fashioned trait, but it is far from that. You might have heard that you shouldn't boast, but then at the same time, everyone around you is boasting. People say you need to be more assertive. Doesn't that go against the grain of being humble? Actually, no. To be strong means standing up for yourself and putting your point of view out not with aggression but with a calm and decisive demeanor. You don't necessarily feel like your opinion is the only opinion that matters, but you feel strongly about it and won't let anyone push you around. That is very compatible with being humble. It is essential in being modest to develop assertiveness.

How can you be humble in your life? Try these exercises to make this happen.

1.   Learn to listen to others, which is key to humility. You show more value to others when you take the time to listen to what others have to say. Plus, having learned the Socratic Method, listening is the number one thing you do when drilling down into an argument. But just being there and being an ear for someone who needs your ear makes you very valuable. The idea is not to solve someone's problems but be a sounding board, a safe place for a friend or family member, or just a total stranger to vent. You will learn more about someone from listening to them rather than speaking to them.

2.   Focus on the present and be mindful. Mindfulness is accepting what is, rather than what you feel it should be. Do not be judgmental. Do not push your opinions on others if you were not asked. But if you do give your opinion, then be gentle with it, so as not to offend, but rather to be constructive. Part of humility is to accept all the faults in yourself. Cut yourself slack if you make a mistake. Don't take it so hard. Mistakes will happen. Learn from them, but don't beat yourself up over them. Always strive to improve yourself. It would be best not to remain stagnant but seek new

opportunities to challenge yourself.

3. Seek feedback from others as it is essential for anyone who wants to be a leader. If you ever take a job where you now find you have the responsibility and are the person in charge, never forget where you came from and how you felt while not on top or in a leadership position. You should seek the feedback of others, whether in person or anonymously, as this can help you make improvements. But then again, don't look to false feedback. Hurtful feedback tends to be thoughtless, so do not take it too seriously. Know which type of feedback is helpful and what is used to get your attention by negative means. Learn this first, and you will do well.

4. Don't use language that is arrogant or filled with pride. It can be challenging to keep from making a snide or vain comment when provoked, but it doesn't make you a better person for doing it. You might want to boast about your accomplishments, which is fine, but try to stay humble. You don't want to show arrogance or show off.

5. We admire humbleness when people don't rave about some great thing they achieved. Reveal your accomplishment, hope people notice your success, and then accept their congratulations with humility and generosity. At the same time, be genuine and honest with others. Don't be envious of someone else's success but learn to see their success to challenge yourself to do better and to be the one to succeed next time. Be humble when it comes to winning and gracious when it comes to losing. Both will be appreciated.

Socrates Warned of Living a Too Busy Life

"Beware the bareness of a busy life."

Much like in our time, when Socrates lived, the men of Athens strove to find fame, fortune, accolades, and political power over a simple life of labor and mediocrity. These desires ruled them. Not much has changed over these last few thousand years, as this is often the primary thing that people still want today.

Athenian men achieved their fame, fortune, and power by keeping busy, always attempting to do more to reach those, sometimes unattainable, goals. And much like when Socrates was alive, people today are similarly engaged. They are always doing something to have their name out in the stratosphere. Whether it is to post on social media, work endless hours, or keep pushing forward to impact society. But all this busyness does not leave people happy. Most people caught up in this cycle are barely satisfied with anything they achieve. They always want more, and enough is never enough. There is no limit, and they don't stop and appreciate what they have.

Socrates lived in contrast to the men of his era. His life was much more straightforward. He did not seek fame, he did not want a large fortune, he was satisfied with his life overall, and he was far happier. He preferred to show others how to lead a simpler life, teach others to think for themselves, and view the wholeness of life rather than the bits and pieces that do not bring satisfaction.

How can you keep from living a busy life? It would help if you lived your life with purpose. It is not essential to care how many likes or "friends" you have. A few good, reliable friends beat the admiration of the empty masses. It is okay not to have fame and fortune. Few people have it as it is, and those that do are isolated. Money and fame do not equal a happy life. Happiness does not come from having "things" but from living a satisfying life of doing good for yourself and others. If you can make someone smile just by stopping and giving someone a boost by telling them a joke, complimenting them, lending them a hand when they are struggling with something, or just being an ear when they feel troubled, you are living a better life.

You have heard the statement "stop and smell the roses," and you might have wondered what that means?

Simply, it is to take time from your life to look around, appreciate those and the world around you, and take a breath. It would help if you reflected on your accomplishments. It would help if you spent time with people you care about and spent time alone, getting to know yourself.
Don't always chase after money, fame, and power.

Try and enjoy the simple things. What you will remember as you move forward in life is not the big things but the small things, like a favorite song, the best cookie you ever ate, the time that you and your friends had fun laughing all night, or a particular conversation you have with your parents or siblings. Those small, seemingly insignificant things are the things that will remain special to your life, not all the significant accomplishments that use up your energy to achieve. Try to remember this as you live your best life.

Socrates Felt that We Need to Be Citizens of The World

"I am not an Athenian or a Greek; I am a citizen of the world."

Socrates lived in a time of real political strife and division. People took sides and were very tribal. This division became even more profound after the Peloponnesian War concluded.

Socrates' view of citizenship was one based on moral and intellectual understanding. These two ideas, combined in their essence, lead to a type of citizenship where one is virtuous because they are actively involved in society and follow its laws. While this idea has not been very influential in most of our societies today, it has influenced the thought of various political philosophers throughout the millennia. So then, what does it mean to be a citizen of the world? How can we interpret what Socrates meant?

Today, we find we need to pick sides. It feels like you can't be on the wrong side, and if you are, you will be the enemy. We also find that we are losing empathy for other people. This lack of empathy is not new. It has always been the case throughout the world at different times in history. But having little empathy towards others who suffer does not bode well for anyone. We all share space on this planet. We are all part of Earth, and we all belong, no matter where we live. We should not be tribal. We need to understand that we are all one because we are all human - regardless of the color of our skin, the place we were born, the language we speak, the culture we grew up in, who we love, what religion we practice or not practice, what we look like, and who we are in essence. Those are just random things and should not separate us.

How do you become a citizen of the world? First, understand that you are part of the world. You are not an island onto yourself. You are one part of the planet, which includes nations and cultures different from your own. Being empathetic to them, and appreciating their differences is part of being a world citizen. Being a citizen of the world engages us and helps us understand what is happening in other parts of the world. We must learn from each other, take care of one another, and strive to be world citizens.

Socrates Felt that We Should Never Seek Revenge

"One should never do wrong in return or mistreat any man, no matter how he has been mistreated."

Socrates felt that any form of revenge or vengeance does more harm than good, even if it seems justified. It ultimately makes the person seeking vengeance less virtuous than the person who perpetrated the need for revenge. He felt all people should be above that.

Revenge is an unjust act used to retaliate against a perceived wrong, but there is no good motivation to justify it. It doesn't make the situation better, and if you get any satisfaction from it, this will only be temporary. It can also backfire and make things worse for you in the long run.

Sometimes, you feel the desire to wreak vengeance and seek retribution when someone has done something to you that made your blood boil or caused you some harm. Doing this might feel good at the moment. We have all heard the term "eye for and eye," and you may feel you are in a situation where you think this is an appropriate solution. But seeking revenge sometimes motivates your so-called "enemies" to retaliate further, and things spiral out of hand. Then every action afterward is tit for tat, and where does that get us?

Harming someone to seek a solution to a bad situation will only worsen that situation. A good example is if you try to discipline a child or a pet by hitting them, you don't teach that child or that pet any lesson except to hit and bite back when they are wronged.

Behaving in this manner is not the way to cope with a bad situation. You don't tear up someone's clothes if they cause you ill. You don't write terrible things on social media to get back at a person who slighted you; you don't destroy the property of someone that might have caused you to lose a job. Doing any of these things, or any other similar revenge act, does not make you better, and you end up only being as bad, if not worse, than the perpetrator.

Socrates was right; we must be above the need to seek vengeance.

If you find yourself in a situation where someone has harmed you, you need to learn to take a breath, walk away, and then calmly reflect on the situation.

Don't spread rumors and lies, and don't do any act that could backfire terribly on you. Instead, become your own advocate.

Stand up for yourself in a calm, decisive way. Act by using legal and responsible methods—rally people to your cause by appealing to their better nature. You will find that by doing this, people will see your side and understand how you were wronged, and they will be willing to help you seek the proper kind of justice rather than vengeance. Then, no matter what, you will be the virtuous and the stronger person, and that alone will make you more powerful, whereas revenge makes you weak.

Socrates Believed That We Should All Have a Sense of Humor

"By all means, marry; if you get a good wife, you will become happy; if you get a bad one, you will become a philosopher."

Socrates was a man who possessed a good sense of humor. He often joked about his wife, as he often sparred with her, and she was one of the few people who challenged him constantly, but his humor about her enabled him to deal with any conflict in his marriage.

The prime reason to hone a good sense of humor is that it helps you cope with complex issues. It breaks it down to its absurdness and lets you release tension. Being able to laugh at yourself enables others to relax around you. It makes you more appealing and approachable. When you find someone charming, the main reason for this is that they don't take themselves too seriously, and they can also make you laugh, bringing you in on the joke. You want to be around people like that as you find you can relate better to them.

Humor and laughter are powerful tools that bring people closer, primarily when used carefully and without malice or bad intentions. Laughter releases stress and helps us cope with life better. Being able to laugh with your friends or family helps improve and strengthen your relationships.

Of course, you don't want to use humor to harm someone. Don't prank someone or use snarky comments to insult someone; that does not elevate your sense of humor; that makes you a jerk. Instead, laugh at the irony of life, bring people in on the joke, and don't take yourself seriously.

In the craziness of this world, you may need to search for the funny. It might not come easy, but it might be necessary to cope with the complex situations we face in life. It is probably one of the most important aspects of being a well-rounded person and one that takes a while for some to develop.

6

—❧—

What are your Takeaways from Socrates?

—❧—

What we know of Socrates, from the words that reflected on this great teacher's life, is that he lived well, surrounded by those who both admired and criticized him. He was authentic and unpretentious, never believing he was above anyone, or they were above him. He remained true to his beliefs, even dying for those beliefs. He imbued his students with a sense of purpose and wonder. They, in turn, shared this with the rest of the world.

Having immersed yourself in the world of Socrates, what lessons will you take away and utilize for your own life?

Hopefully, you will examine who you are and what you would like to be and challenge yourself to lead a more open and better life by following some of Socrates' ideas, especially when it comes to critical thinking. Make yourself a citizen of the world, use the Socratic Method to question flawed concepts, and learn to be a more well-rounded individual.

Let the teachings of Socrates guide you throughout your life.

BIBLIOGRAPHY

En.wikipedia.org. 2022. *Socrates - Wikipedia*. [online] Available at: <https://en.wikipedia.org/wiki/Socrates>

p.utm.edu. 2022. *Socrates | Internet Encyclopedia of Philosophy*. [online] Available at: <https://iep.utm.edu/socrates/>

Plato.stanford.edu. 2022. *Socrates (Stanford Encyclopedia of Philosophy)*. [online] Available at: <https://plato.stanford.edu/entries/socrates/>

Goodreads.com. 2022. *Socrates Quotes (Author of Apología de Sócrates)*. [online] Available at: https://www.goodreads.com/author/quotes/275648.Socrates

Culture. 2022. *Socrates—facts and information*. [online] Available at: <https://www.nationalgeographic.com/culture/article/socrates>

ThoughtCo. 2022. *A Profile of Socrates, Ancient Philosopher and Sage*. [online] Available at: <https://www.thoughtco.com/profile-of-socrates-121053>

Teach Anywhere. 2022. *The Socratic Method*. [online] Available at: <https://teachanywhere.byu.edu/teaching-tips/the-socratic-method>

Law.uchicago.edu. 2022. *The Socratic Method | University of Chicago Law School*. [online] Available at: <https://www.law.uchicago.edu/socratic-method>

BrainyQuote. 2022. *Socrates Quotes - BrainyQuote*. [online] Available at:<https://www.brainyquote.com/authors/socrates-quotes>

ILLUSTRATIONS:

Illustration 227056443 © Rudzhan Nagiev | Dreamstime.com

Illustration 108251834 © Mimomy | Dreamstime.com

Illustration 225459607 © Alexlmx | Dreamstime.com

If You Enjoyed This Book, Please Leave a Review on

Amazon.com, B&N, and Smashwords

Please Look for These Books in the Be a Great Thinker Series:

Book 1 – Introduction to Critical Thinking
Book 3 – Plato – The Father of Western Philosophy

And Be Sure to Look for Other Books to be Released Soon in this Series!

ABOUT THE AUTHORS

Adrienne Roth and Matthew Roth are passionate about Philosophy and Critical Thinking. They have spent their lives exploring ways to quantify their arguments, questioning flawed ideas, and trying to bring people together through truth and reality. This book series wants to show young adults how to do the same in their lives.

www.ingramcontent.com/pod-product-compliance
Lightning Source LLC
Chambersburg PA
CBHW070452130626
46553CB00006B/2366